FIND YOUR RAINBOW

Inspirations for *Children*

COMPILED AND WRITTEN BY PATRICIA OVERSON

ISBN 13: 978-1-59298-503-6

Library of Congress Catalog Number: 2012909941

Printed in the United States of America
First Printing: 2012

16 15 14 13 12   5 4 3 2 1

Cover and interior design by James Monroe Design, LLC.

Beaver's Pond Press, Inc.
7108 Ohms Lane
Edina, MN 55439–2129
(952) 829-8818
www.BeaversPondPress.com

To order, visit www.BeaversPondBooks.com
or call (800) 901-3480. Reseller discounts available.

findyourrainbow123@gmail.com
www.findyourrainbow123.com

Every effort has been made to trace the ownership of all material included in this book and to secure necessary permissions to reprint these selections. The author regrets any inadvertent omission or error and will make any necessary corrections in future printings.

PERMISSIONS

The author wishes to express her thanks to the following authors or publishers, or their authorized representatives, for their kind permission to reprint their works:

Leni Erickson: "Children, You Are a Gift" © 2012 by Leni Erickson. Reprinted by permission of the poet. www.lenierickson.com

Catherine Pulsifer: "Allow Yourself" © 2009 by Catherine Pulsifer. Reprinted by permission of the poet. www.wow4u.com

Quote by Jim Rohn, America's Foremost Business Philosopher, reprinted with permission from Jim Rohn International © 2011. www.JimRohn.com

To:

_____

From:

_____

Date:

_____

Introduction

Encouragement and advice. Inspiration and wisdom. One generation to another.

With *Find Your Rainbow: Inspirations for Children*, I invite you to create lasting connections with the children in your life. Whether they are younger or older, related to you by birth or by circumstance, they will treasure this collection of well-chosen words—given and personalized by someone who cares enough to share insights and experience gained through the years.

In this volume, I have included reflections and words to live by from figures ranging from Albert Einstein to Maya Angelou. The collection offers ideas to linger over, to ponder, and to save. All have had meaning in my life.

I have also offered my own writings—poems and brief perspectives—that I hope readers will find insightful and influential.

My desire for this collection is that it opens the pathway from one generation to the next, presenting opportunities for conversation to strengthen our connecting stories. With that in mind, I hope you will personalize the book before you give it as a gift.

You can customize it in two ways: Check the box next to any of the heartfelt messages and poems to note that the sentiment particularly resonates with you, or write personal thoughts or heartfelt memories on the blank pages provided at the end of the book. You can even include favorite photographs.

Giving this keepsake will help communicate your values, beliefs, and wisdom in a unique way. And these personalized pages can be revisited and treasured year after year, for generations to come.

I hope you will let this remarkable collection become part of your legacy.

~ Patricia Overson

Dream lofty dreams, and as you dream, so shall you become.
Your vision is the promise of what you shall one day be;
your ideal is the prophecy of what you shall at last unveil.

~ James Allen

Every great dream begins with a dreamer.
Always remember, you have within you the strength,
the patience, and the passion
to reach for the stars to change the world.

~ Harriet Tubman

It takes courage to listen to your dreams,
confidence to believe in your dreams,
determination to act on your dreams,
and persistence to achieve your dreams.

~ Patricia Overson

Find Your Rainbow, Precious Child

Rainbow, rainbow—oh, to find you a rainbow!
Precious child, I would catch a rainbow just for you.
And when your world is cloudy,
Its arc of brilliant colors
Would bring you a promise of hope.

Rainbow, rainbow—oh, to find you a rainbow!
Such a glorious wonder!
Where the skies hold a promise just for you.
I would find that place, fetch that rainbow,
And release its magical colors to paint your innermost dreams.

Rainbow, rainbow—oh, to find you a rainbow!
If I could take your dark clouds,
I would send them beyond the rainbow,
Far away, where they would never return,
And encourage you to realize your rainbow dreams.

Rainbow, rainbow—you will find your rainbow.
This wisdom I offer to you:
Never let go of your rainbow dreams,
Never settle for anything less
Than what you aspire to be.

Always remember:
The storms will pass,
The rainbow will follow,
The skies will again be blue.
And I will always be there, just for you.

~ Patricia Overson

*I could not point to any need in childhood
as strong as that for a father's protection.*

~ Sigmund Freud

Our truest life is when we are in dreams awake.

~ Henry David Thoreau

Dig deep into your soul and plant a dream.

~ Patricia Overson

This is my wish for you:
Comfort on difficult days,
smiles when sadness intrudes,
rainbows to follow the clouds,
laughter to kiss your lips,
sunsets to warm your heart,
hugs when spirits sag,
beauty for your eyes to see,
friendships to brighten your being,
faith so that you can believe,
confidence for when you doubt,
courage to know yourself,
patience to accept the truth,
love to complete your life.

~ Author Unknown

Aim for success, not perfection. . . .
Never give up your right to be wrong
because then you will lose the ability
to learn new things and to move forward with your life.

~ Dr. David D. Burns

First, say to yourself what you would be;
and then do what you have to do.

~ Epictetus

When you have a rainbow deep in your soul,
your light will reveal your spirit.
Share that radiant awareness with others.

~ Patricia Overson

The important thing is
not to stop questioning.
Curiosity has its own reason for existence.
One cannot help but be
in awe when he contemplates
the mysteries of eternity,
of life,
of the marvelous structure of reality.
It is enough if one tries merely to
comprehend a little of this mystery each day.

~ Albert Einstein

Jump into the middle of things,
get your hands dirty,
fall flat on your face,
and then reach for the stars.

~ Joan L. Curcio

A dream is in the mind of the believer
and in the hands of the doer.
You are not given a dream without
being given the power to make it come true.

~ Anonymous

Beloved child, hold on to your rainbow dreams.
Seek them, believe in them, and they will find you.

~ Patricia Overson

Children, You Are a Gift

We love being with you.

Your endless enthusiasm warms our hearts.
Your vibrant spirit delights those worn thin
    with time.
Your fresh perception beckons us to look
    again.

We love being with you.

Your boundless energy pulses us with life
    anew.
Your infinite imagination widens outlooks
    gone narrow.
Your countless inquiries free our creative
    spirit.

We love being with you.

You touch us deeply, truly, honestly.
You warm hearts.
You make souls dance.
You spark spirits.
You enjoy life.

We love being with you.

In being purely present, you give so much so
    effortlessly.

We love being with you.

~ Leni Erickson

You cannot change the circumstances,
the seasons, or the wind,
but you can change yourself.

~ Jim Rohn

The work will wait while you show the child the rainbow,
but the rainbow won't wait while you do the work.

~ Patricia Clafford

You only have one life on this earth;
live it with all your heart and soul.

~ Patricia Overson

Always Have Faith in Yourself

Know yourself and all of your unique qualities.
You have so much to offer, so much to do, and so much to consider.
You have the ability to achieve whatever you seek.
Always have faith in yourself!

Aim higher than you believe you can reach.
Choose carefully, for you will get what you pursue.
Understand who you are and what you want to be.
Always have faith in yourself!

Be yourself, because God created the perfect you.
Let everything you do reflect honesty, faithfulness, and joy.
You have the strength to take control of your circumstances in life.
Always have faith in yourself!

Believe in your power, your purpose, and your potential.
Let nothing hold you back from exploring your aspirations and dreams.
Remember, you are the master designer of your world.
Always have faith in yourself!

~ Patricia Overson

Wake up with a smile and go after life. . . .
Live it, enjoy it,
taste it, smell it,
feel it.

~ Joe Kapp

Walk on a rainbow trail;
walk on a trail of song,
and all about you will be beauty.
There is a way out of every dark mist,
over a rainbow trail.

~ Navajo Quote

Who you are and what you do matters.
Recognize your gifts and fulfill your purpose in life.

~ Patricia Overson

A mature person is one who
does not think only in absolutes,
who is able to be objective even
when deeply stirred emotionally,
who has learned that there is both good and bad
in all people and all things,
and who walks humbly and deals charitably
with the circumstances of life,
knowing that in this world no one
is all-knowing and therefore all of us
need both love and charity.

~ Eleanor Roosevelt

No person has the right to rain on your dreams.

~ Marian Wright Edelman

*Just as angels are attracted to
the light of joy and kindness,
so too are miracles attracted to
the lamp of faith and love.*

~ Mary Augustine

*It is not enough to have a dream
unless you're willing to chase it with urgency.
Look past the dreariest clouds and seek the promise of the rainbow.
You must follow wherever your dream leads.*

~ Patricia Overson

Allow Yourself

Allow yourself to dream
And when you do dream big.

Allow yourself to learn
And when you do learn all you can.

Allow yourself to laugh
And when you do share your laughter.

Allow yourself to set goals
And when you do reward yourself as you
    move forward.

Allow yourself to be determined
And when you do you will find you will
    succeed.

Allow yourself to believe in yourself
And when you do you will find
    self-confidence.

Allow yourself to lend a helping hand
And when you do a hand will help you.

Allow yourself relaxation
And when you do you will find new ideas.

Allow yourself love
And when you do you will find love in
    return.

Allow yourself to be happy
And when you do you will influence others
    around you.

Allow yourself to be positive
And when you do life will get easier.

~ Catherine Pulsifer

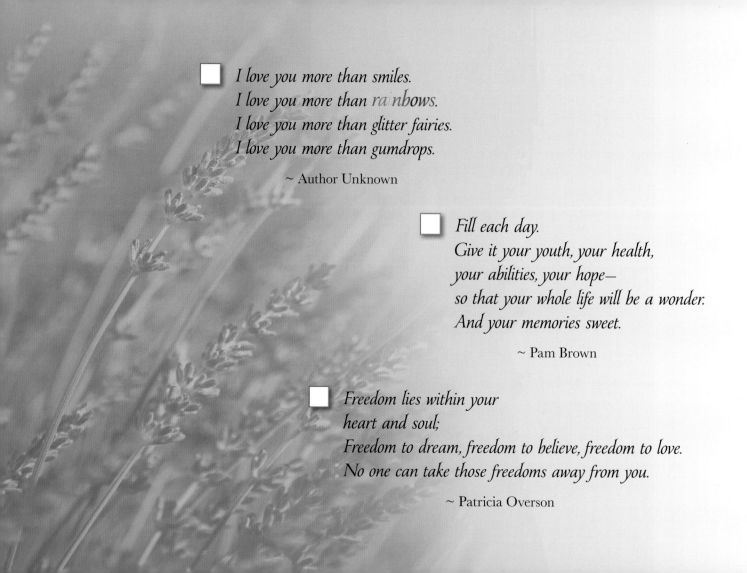

I love you more than smiles.
I love you more than rainbows.
I love you more than glitter fairies.
I love you more than gumdrops.

~ Author Unknown

Fill each day.
Give it your youth, your health,
your abilities, your hope—
so that your whole life will be a wonder.
And your memories sweet.

~ Pam Brown

Freedom lies within your
heart and soul;
Freedom to dream, freedom to believe, freedom to love.
No one can take those freedoms away from you.

~ Patricia Overson

Life Is for Living

Life is a gift we're given each and every day.
Dream about tomorrow, but live for today.
To live a little, you've got to love a whole lot.
Love turns the ordinary into the extraordinary.

Life's a journey
always worth taking.
Take time to smell the roses... and tulips...
and daffodils... and lilacs... and
  sunflowers...

Count blessings like children count stars.
The secret of a happy life isn't buried in a
treasure chest ... it lies within your heart.

It's the little moments that make life big.
Don't wait. Make memories today.

Celebrate your life!

~ Author Unknown

The moment of enlightenment
is when a person's
dreams of possibilities
become images of probabilities.

~ Vic Braden

What a privilege to be here on the planet
to contribute your unique donation to humankind.
Each face in the rainbow of colors that populate our
world is precious and special.

~ Morris Dees

To achieve great things,
know your purpose,
act on your dreams,
and believe in possibilities.

~ Patricia Overson

Live for something.
Do good and leave behind you a monument
of virtue that the storm of time can never destroy.
Write your name, in kindness, love, and mercy,
on the hearts of thousands you come in contact
with, year by year: you will never be forgotten.
No, your name, your deeds will be as legible
on the hearts you leave behind as the stars
on the brow of evening.
Good deeds will shine as the stars of heaven.

~ Thomas Chalmers

Try to be a rainbow in someone's cloud.

~ Maya Angelou

Never be bullied into silence.
Never allow yourself to be made a victim.
Accept no one's definition of your life;
define yourself.

~ Harvey Fierstein

Be careful of people who tell you who you are
or who you should be.
Be yourself, and contribute
something magnificent to the world
that will make a difference.

~ Patricia Overson

If You Have a Dream

If you have a dream,
Do whatever it takes to make your dream
   come true.
The wondrous dream you believe in
Can become a reality.

If you have a dream,
Be mindful of your thoughts, your beliefs,
   and your destiny.
Listen patiently to your inner voice and
   trust your instincts.
Don't let the world distract you.

If you have a dream,
Reach for the stars, for the dream you can
   call your own.
Have the conviction that any dream is
   possible.
Dream with confidence and determination.

If you have a dream,
Hold it in your heart and mind and never
   let it go.
Lift your hopes toward heaven and know
   that God will guide you.
Have faith that you will attain your dream.

~ Patricia Overson

☐ *Keep your dreams alive.*
Understand to achieve anything requires faith and belief in yourself,
vision, hard work, determination, and dedication.
Remember all things are possible for those who believe.

~ Gail Devers

☐ *There are many wonderful things that will never be done if you do not do them.*

~ Charles D. Gill

☐ *Aim toward the sun;*
reach into your soul,
and find your rainbow.
Let it shine bright.

~ Patricia Overson

When you are inspired by some great purpose,
some extraordinary project,
all your thoughts break their bonds:
your mind transcends limitations,
your consciousness expands in every direction,
and you find yourself in a new, great, and wonderful world.
Dormant forces, faculties, and talents become alive,
and you discover yourself to be a greater person by far
than you ever dreamed yourself to be.

~ Patanjali

The soul would have no rainbow had the eyes no tears.

~ John Vance Cheney

Fear less, hope more;
eat less, chew more;
whine less, breathe more;
talk less, say more;
hate less, love more;
and all good things are yours.

~ Swedish Proverb

Take time to be quiet and listen to God's whispers,
before He has to shake you with a shout.

~ Patricia Overson

Life's Mirror

There are loyal hearts, there are spirits brave
There are souls that are pure and true.
Then give to the world the best you have
And the best will come back to you.

Give love, and love to your life will flow,
A strength in its utmost need.
Have faith, and a score of hearts will show
Their faith in your word and deed.

Give truth, and your gift will be paid in kind
And honor will honor meet;
And a smile that is sweet will surely find
A smile that is just as sweet!

Give pity and sorrow to those that mourn,
You will gather in flowers again;
The scattered seeds from your thought outborne
Though the sowing seemed but vain.

For life is the mirror of king and slave
It is just what we are, and do.
Then give to the world the best that you have
And the best will come back to you!

~ Madeline S. Bridges

The first step toward getting somewhere is to decide that you are not going to stay where you are.

~ John J.B. Morgan and Ewing T. Webb

Don't let anyone rob you of your imagination,
your creativity, or your curiosity.
It's your place in the world; it's your life.
Go on and do all you can with it,
and make it the life you want to live.

~ Mae Jemison

God knows the purpose He has for you;
allow Him to guide you toward it.

~ Patricia Overson

May flowers always line your path
And sunshine light your day.
May songbirds serenade you
Every step along the way.

May a rainbow run beside you
In a sky that's always blue.
And may happiness fill your heart
Each day your whole life through.

~ Irish Blessing

*God put the rainbow in the clouds themselves so that
in the worst of times,
in the meanest of times,
in the dreariest of times,
so that at all times the viewer can see a possibility of hope.*

~ Maya Angelou

*Everyone needs and deserves love and happiness.
Let's not wait until we're perfect to go out and find it.*

~ Pat A. Mitchell

*Life's purpose is to:
Give back more than we have taken;
Be accountable for our actions;
Be faithful to God and the ones we love;
And be charitable in meeting the needs of others.*

~ Patricia Overson

Listen to your life.
See it for the fathomless mystery that it is.
In the boredom and pain of it no less
than in the excitement and gladness:
touch, taste, smell your way to the holy
and hidden heart of it because in the last analysis
all moments are key moments,
and life itself is grace.

~ Frederick Buechner

Life is full of beauty.
Notice it.
Notice the bumble bee,
the small child, and the smiling faces.
Smell the rain, and feel the wind.
Live your life to the fullest potential,
and fight for your dreams.

~ Ashley Smith

They may run, walk, stumble, drive, or fly,
but they never lose sight of the reason for the journey,
and they never miss a chance to see a rainbow on the way.

~ Gloria Gaither

The best legacy you can give a child is:
Empowerment—I accept who you are;
Honesty—I honor your word;
Trust—I believe in your truth.

~ Patricia Overson

Child

Listen to your dreams, child—listen with intensity!
Nothing is impossible for those who have faith.

Promise yourself, child, to be who you are meant to be.
If you want to accomplish this, you have to believe it first.

If you falter, child, don't let discouragement stop you.
Forget the "I can't" and do what you can.

Don't let the naysayers get you down, child.
When you trust in your dreams and believe in yourself,
Your hopes can become your reality.

~ Patricia Overson

Personal Thoughts from My Heart

Personal Thoughts from My Heart

_____

_____

_____

_____

_____

_____

_____

_____

_____

Photos from My Heart

Photos from My Heart

About the Author: Patricia Overson has spent years exploring the world, feeding her passion to see and learn about new people, places, and cultures. Whether she's photographing a family of lions on a safari in South Africa or pondering the majesty of the Grand Canyon, Patricia has gleaned a wealth of knowledge and life experience.

Now she is taking that passion a step further and is sharing with others some of the things she has learned along the way. Patricia's hope is that through the passages in this book, she will sow seeds of encouragement in the lives of her readers. Such encouragement, she believes, can blossom into inspiration, hope, and the confidence to turn dreams into realities.

Patricia and her husband, John, enjoy traveling together. They have two grown children and are delighted to be grandparents. They live in a suburb of Minneapolis, Minnesota.

Acknowledgements: With special thanks to my publisher, Beaver's Pond Press, project mentor Lily Coyle, and designer James Monroe; my team of editors, Sharon Emery, Sharon Hodge, and Nancy B. Olsen; and my legal team, attorney Aaron Young and his assistant, law student Maggie Armstrong. It is with a grateful heart that I thank my children, Jason and Kristine, and granddaughter, Bella Patricia Overson, who inspire me; and my supportive husband, John, who read draft after draft and who never fails to offer encouragement and wise feedback.

Also by Patricia Overson: *Find Your Rainbow: Inspirations for Grandchildren* (Beaver's Pond Press, 2012)